# *THE KNACK OF USING YOUR SUBCONSCIOUS MIND*

# *THE KNACK OF USING*

# *YOUR*

# *SUBCONSCIOUS MIND*

*By* John K. Williams

PRENTICE-HALL, Inc.
Englewood Cliffs, N.J. 07632

This book is available at a special discount
when ordered in bulk quantities. Contact
Prentice-Hall, Inc., General Publishing Division,
Special Sales, Englewood Cliffs, N.J. 07632.



10 9 8 7 6 5 4 3 2 1



Prentice-Hall International, Inc., *London*
Prentice-Hall of Australia Pty. Limited, *Sydney*
Prentice-Hall Canada Inc., *Toronto*
Prentice-Hall of India Private Limited, *New Delhi*
Prentice-Hall of Japan, Inc., *Tokyo*
Prentice-Hall of Southeast Asia Pte. Ltd., *Singapore*
Editora Prentice-Hall do Brasil Ltda., *Rio de Janeiro*

Library of Congress Catalog Card Number: 52-7757

ISBN 0-13-516492-3 (A REWARD BOOK : PBK.)

PRINTED IN THE UNITED STATES OF AMERICA

51650

*To Lily and Anne*

## TABLE OF CHAPTERS

# PREFACE

ONLY in comparatively recent years have men and women in business and the professions, and students in our colleges and universities, begun to suspect the power and usefulness of the subconscious mind. Surprisingly little has been written about its functioning except in treatises on psychology; and its practical use in connection with the activities and demands of daily living seems to be understood by few people.

This is unfortunate, for the subconscious mind is an extremely efficient and dependable working partner, capable of solving many of our most baffling problems and of creating bold new ideas for our personal growth and progress.

Uncannily successful in grappling with the knotty problems of business and the professions, the subconscious mind is equally effective in helping us to arrive at wise plans and decisions in our personal affairs—our home problems, the bringing up of our children, our church, club and social activities, our community life, and our relations with the world at large. Its ideas and solutions are usually more creative than those worked out by our conscious mental processes. Yet we are inclined to regard the subconscious mind—when we give it any thought at all—as a sort of psychological stepchild.

The author's aim is to reveal the power and importance of this creative silent partner, and to show how it may be used to increase our effectiveness and enrich our lives. If, in his endeavor to make the subject understandable, he has been guilty of over-simplification, perhaps that fault will be excused in a book that lays no claim to being scientific but is intended to be as practical and helpful as possible to the average reader.

Included by permission are portions of chapters from a book long out of print, *The Subconscious Mind in Business*, by Robert R. Updegraff. These contributions to the present text are acknowledged with deep appreciation.

Without further delay, the reader is invited to enter and explore the most fascinating realm in the world—his own mind.

*THE KNACK OF USING*

*YOUR*

*SUBCONSCIOUS MIND*

CHAPTER I

# *Our Silent Partner, the Subconscious Mind*

ALL of us can, if we desire, tap an unsuspected source of pure energy and creative power. This source, fully adequate and freely available, is our silent partner—the subconscious area of our mind.

While the role of the subconscious mind is not new, only in recent years have we come to appreciate the true importance that subconscious activity can play in an individual's success and progress. Yet from the time of Socrates, the founder of ethical science, to the inventive genius of Edison, Ford, Marconi, Westinghouse, Einstein and Kettering, this little-understood field of mental activity has delivered the insight and know-how for almost every great achievement in science, industry and the arts. It is with the workings of this deeper area of the mind that we are concerned.

Modern psychology confirms the existence of the subconscious area of mind. The conscious mind is just the "emergent apex," the top level of an enormous and sustaining subconscious. Research has shown that the ability to bring into action subconscious mental activity determines the success of every creative worker—scientist, author, musician, inventor or business leader.

The average business or professional man has little or no conception of the tremendous power that lies concealed and unused in the area of mind below the level of consciousness. By correctly using this potential, we can gain release from tension and frustration and have at our disposal abundant energy and new mental power and physical well-being.

These things we gain without striving. There is no laborious routine to follow. We simply recognize our subconscious mind and permit it to function under proper conditions.

* * *

Observe the working habits of leaders in any field and you will find that important discoveries are seldom made while engaged actively in research investigation. New insight, bold ideas and plans, are contributed by the underlying activity of mind—the subconscious function.

The noted German scientist, von Helmholtz, when speaking to a group of friends on his seventieth birthday said: "Happy ideas come unexpectedly, without effort, like an inspiration, so far as I am concerned. They have never come to me when my mind was fatigued or when I was at my working table." The French mathematician, Henri Poincare, described his creative work in almost the same terms. He stated that creative ideas did not come to him while he worked at his desk, but frequently flashed into his mind while he engaged in other activities.

William Blake, the English artist and poet, did his immortal work while his subconscious was in complete control. The poet, Coleridge, developed in detail his great poem, *Kubla Khan,* while his confused conscious mind was under the influence of an opiate. Tschaikowsky, the composer, said, "The germ of a future composition comes suddenly and unexpectedly."

Every successful businessman as well as every creative thinker knows the experience Lamartine had in mind when he said, "It is not I who think. It is my ideas that think for me." Mozart was recalling the same kind of subconscious mental activity when he wrote to a friend, "The process with me is like a vivid dream."

Christopher Morley, the writer, found that many of his best ideas came to him while reclining on a davenport reading detective stories, his conscious mind completely absorbed in the tales.

Elbert Hubbard declared that his most important ideas came to him while working in the garden or riding horseback.

Harvey made his discovery of the circulation of the blood as the result of subconscious mental activity.[1] Dr. Walter B. Cannon discovered the significance of bodily changes in fear and rage when, "one wakeful night . . . the idea flashed through my mind."[2]

The subconscious picks its own times and places. Modern civilization enjoys rail locomotion because James Watt, who invented the steam engine, took a quiet walk one Sunday afternoon. "I was thinking of the engine at the time. . . . I had not walked further

[1] *An Anatomical Discussion on the Nature of the Heart and Blood in Animals*, translated by Robert Willis, London 1847.

[2] *The Way of an Investigator*, by Walter B. Cannon, W. W. Norton & Co., 1945.

than the golf house when the whole thing was arranged in my mind."[3]

The theory of evolution is embedded in the very fabric of modern thought. For many years Charles Darwin through intensive and unremitting observation had accumulated data which he felt pointed to a new and significant insight. In a brief autobiographical statement he says, "I can remember the very spot in the road, whilst in my carriage, when to my joy the whole solution came to me."[4] Interestingly enough, A. R. Wallace, who shares with Darwin the achievement of discovering the theory of evolution, had his first clear idea in his bed during an attack of malaria.

The most momentous concept of this age, the relationship of time and space and the nature of reality sprang into the mind of Albert Einstein while confined to his bed because of illness. Who can say but for this period of enforced quiet and relaxation this world may not have been blessed (or cursed) by the atom bomb.

The subconscious area of the mind is an unplumbed reservoir of creative insight and intuition. Inventors

[3] *History of Mechanical Inventions*, by Abbot P. Usher, McGraw-Hill Co., 1929.

[4] *The Art of Scientific Investigation*, by W. I. B. Beveridge, W. W. Norton & Co., 1950.

and scientists engaged in research know this to be true. In a recent survey of the working habits of French scientists, seventy-five per cent of those investigated stated that important discoveries never came to them while they were consciously engaged in research investigation. Their discoveries were contributed by the inner, underlying activity of mind—the subconscious function. The same result was found when Joseph Rossman, a prominent American patent lawyer, studied the creative thinking of several hundred inventors.[5]

Progress comes from the "supersense" found only in the subconscious. These inspirational uprushes come during periods of relaxation following intense conscious application to the problem.

Many business and professional men get their best ideas when shaving in the morning. Many mothers arrive at happy solutions to their home and family problems while dressing or combing their hair. There is nothing accidental about this phenomenon. It represents the working of the subconscious mind and is characteristic of its operation.

Many men and women who have achieved promi-

[5] *The Basic Teachings of Great Psychologists*, S. Stansfeld Sargent, Ph.D., Barnes & Noble.

nence in business, the professions and the arts, owe much of their success to the use of their subconscious minds—without ever realizing it. They might have been even more successful had they been familiar with the rules for using this highly creative function of the mind, and consciously enlisted its help, with the confidence that comes from understanding.

While admittedly we know far too little as yet about the why and how of our subconscious mental processes, we do know that the subconscious mind can be used consciously with results that are little short of amazing. There are certain methods that can be learned. It is the mission of this book to explain these methods.

It would be a mistake to attempt to use the mechanics of this function of the mind without some understanding of the inter-relationship of both the conscious and subconscious areas of the mind, and of how each complements and is dependent upon the other. Hence the subject is approached in this volume from the broad angle of the creative power of the mind as a whole, narrowing down in the end to the practical "knack" of using the subconscious function—for there is a certain knack to it.

CHAPTER 2

# *The Unlimited Creative Power of the Mind*

IT IS not necessary for an individual to have technical training in the field of psychology to understand and appreciate the unlimited creative power of the human mind. There are, however, certain facts which, if kept in view, will enable each of us to use our mind in a more intelligent, purposeful way. As a foundation for such an understanding, a brief statement regarding the two aspects of mind is essential.

People who are expert in the field of psychology have long recognized that mind has two phases or functions, or, perhaps more correctly stated, two ways of expressing itself. These two aspects of mind are called the *conscious mind* and the *subconscious mind.* Some speak of these two phases of mind as the *objective mind* and the *subjective mind.*

For the purpose of this book the terms conscious mind and subconscious mind will be employed. The use of these terms in no way indicates that we possess two minds. Mind is one, not plural. It is a unity and functions as such. There are, however, two different fields of operation or levels of work involved in our mental processes.

Let us first consider that aspect of mind known as the conscious or objective mind. This is the part of mind which makes decisions and exercises the power of choice. It has the ability to select, to discriminate between what is desired and what is not desired. It is that part of mind which sits in judgment. It determines what we want or desire, and it initiates action to secure results. The conscious mind knows persons, things and conditions.

The significant thing about the conscious mind, it should be stressed, is its selectivity, or power of choice and decision. By its own nature, and because of this nature, the conscious mind can decide what it wants to think, what it wants to achieve, and how it will respond to other minds. It is the supreme determining and selecting power of personality.

In ordinary language, the conscious mind is that

which one speaks of when a person speaks of his "self." But a fuller understanding will indicate that the conscious mind is not the total self but only one aspect of self or personality.

* * *

Every object or condition must first exist in the mind. Before any idea or plan can be formed, or any result achieved, it must first exist as an idea or concept in the conscious mind. Whether we realize it or not, all our lives we live and work to a series of mental pictures or blueprints. Making blueprints is the function of the conscious mind. In the exercise of this power the direction and content of one's life is determined.

Before a bridge is built the architect must make a blueprint. Every detail of the proposed structure, its location, its size and weight, its relation to its surroundings, the material of which it is to be built—all these are visualized completely and in detail in the mind of the architect and reduced to a blueprint before the engineers begin the process of construction.

This is not only true of bridges and buildings; it is true of everything that comes into, and forms a part of our lives. In general terms, the conscious mind may be thought of as the architect and the subconscious mind as the construction engineer.

The conscious mind may not know how the subconscious works or feels, but the subconscious knows, to the last detail and shade of feeling, just what is in the conscious mind. The subconscious may overflow and trick the conscious mind, but the reverse is never true. The conscious mind must first honestly feel and believe that larger wisdom and insight can find the solution. The method—the how and the why of the answer—is the responsibility of the subconscious mind.

Teamed up, the two functions of mind present us with limitless opportunity for achievement and growth.

## CHAPTER 3

# *First Requisite for Creative Mental Life*

EVERY experience or condition of our life —success or failure, prosperity or penury, progress or frustration, growth or stagnation—is the result of an action or process selected and set in motion by our conscious mind. But to develop our full powers, it is necessary that we learn to use the creative power of *both* functions of our mind, consciously, continuously, and intelligently.

Simply because mental and emotional activity—or thought and feeling processes—cannot be measured in terms of height, length, width or weight is no reason for assuming that these activities are not real in a definite and concrete sense. A thought expressed or projected becomes an enduring part of the personality from which it goes forth. In fact, it helps to create and crystallize that personality. Further, it becomes a part of the individual's world.

Mind is creative, but it must have some objective or blueprint to which it can work. Mental activity provides the power for attainment. Every condition, every experience of life, is the result of our mental and emotional activity. We can do only what we *think* we can do. We can have only what we *think* we can have. Everything we do and are and have is the result of thought. We never express anything that we do not first have in our mind. Hence, the secret of attainment, of progress, of developing a creative personality, is found in constructive mental and emotional activity.

The external world is but a reflection of the world within us. Whatever is imaged in our inner life will be reflected in our personal world. Our mental and emotional activity, focused on a desire—a picture in our mind—will supply us with limitless energy, and will take whatever form our mind demands.

It is not only true that we are free to select positive or negative thoughts, but, by the very nature of life, we *must* do so. Thoughts of personal growth and progress, of earning a good income, of having influence with people, of experiencing satisfaction in our work and our daily life—the things we call success and happiness—reflect themselves in time in the conditions under which we work and live. Thoughts of doubt, frustration, failure and personal limitations operate in precisely the same fashion.

The first requisite of creative mental life is, therefore, positive thinking. Aspiration molds the mind in a stronger way than does fear or trepidation. Appreciation is more creative than aversion. Confident thoughts are more powerful than questioning doubts. It is by thoughts of high desire and hope—emotions that are courageous and inspiring—that we achieve more abundant and creative living, a more harmonious inner state and a more commanding personality.

It is important for us to realize that personality is not something one is endowed with at birth, as one is given legs or a liver or a heart. It is something that is being constantly created, day after day, as one lives life. Whether that personality shall be colorful or insipid, barren or productive, a source of frustration and misery or a storehouse of power, depends upon the thoughts one cultivates, the ideas and ideals one entertains, the emotions one enjoys and therefore encourages.

We are not limited by the kind of person we are today. We can reshape our life through the creative power of mind. For what mind has formed it can unform. The individual who wants for his inner companion a personality that has poise, strength, influence, and spiritual power must cultivate these qualities continuously. By conscious effort he must control his thinking and his emotions. The ideal personality is never satisfied with itself as it is, or with things as they are. It grows daily through the creative power of mind, understood and used.

Our conscious thoughts, empowered by strong feelings, are a creative force. Positive, constructive, purposeful, confident thoughts will gradually reproduce themselves in the actual conditions of a person's life.

The underlying purpose of this book is to create understanding of this creative power, and to suggest practical ways for its use.

CHAPTER 4

# *The Mind We Do Not Know and Seldom Use*

WHEN the average individual is told that mind has unlimited power available for its use, the statement is usually passed off as high-pressure "inspiration." But the facts of everyday experience prove that the human mind actually has amazing powers, which few of us ever draw upon, so slight is our knowledge, and so limited is our faith.

The easiest thing in the world is to drift without purpose or direction, so far as our thoughts and feelings are concerned. When we do this we are letting the creative powers of mind go to waste.

Modern science is based on controlled experimentation and observation. The only way any person can know whether or not mind does have unlimited power available for its use is for that person to test the idea by actual personal experience. An experiment carried on for a sufficient period of time is all that is needed. It is not a matter that can be demonstrated in a week or a month, as a rule, for only occasionally do we experience prompt proof. But, given time, each of us can prove the power of mind for himself. It may require faith and perseverance, but the rewards will be great.

It is true that one of the most difficult things in the world for any individual to do is to control his own thinking and his own feelings. We are all influenced by habitual tendencies of thought and limited by emotional attitudes based on childhood experiences and accumulated prejudices, by other individuals, and by external conditions, to such an extent that comparatively few of us achieve any degree of sustained control over our mental and emotional processes. That is, unless we work at it consciously and persistently—*and utilize the subconscious function of our mind.*

The trouble is, few of us have become acquainted with this area of our mind, and learned the technique of using it; so we have not proved to ourselves that mind is, in very fact, the originating and determining influence in all that we are and all that we have.

In order to make the issue definite and concrete, consider the following statement: *Any idea, plan or purpose may be planted in the subconscious mind by repetition of thought, empowered by faith and expectancy.*

Can this statement be demonstrated to be true through experimentation and observation?

Is there any known method or technique by which the proof may be secured?

If there is such a method or technique, is it available to everyone?

These questions can all be answered with an emphatic "Yes."

To understand the method by which any person may test, through actual experience, the correctness of this statement, it will be necessary to consider briefly the nature of this little-understood area of our mind.

The subconscious area is that part which lies below the level of consciousness or memory. It is the great storehouse or reservoir of all our past thoughts, attitudes and desires. Into its millions of pigeonholes go the things we read, hear, observe; the pictures we see, the impressions we receive, the thoughts we entertain as we go about our daily life. Hence the field of our subconscious mind is many times greater than that of our conscious mind. It is constantly accumulating the material for a broader, fuller, richer life than most of us have learned to live.

* * *

There are two significant facts regarding the subconscious mind that are little understood, hence are unappreciated and unused by most of us. The first is that the subconscious mind contains within itself the power to *create*. The second is that the subconscious mind can be made to obey the orders given to it by the conscious mind. For, unlike the conscious mind, the subconscious mind has no power of choice. By its very nature it must do what it is told to do. Its function or purpose is that of bringing to full expression whatever is desired by the higher or self-conscious aspect of our mind.

A simple but helpful analogy is that of charging an electric storage battery. You have a given structure—the cells and necessary chemicals—which receives the current from the generator. The battery accepts the charge of electricity from the generator because it is that kind of instrument. In personality you have a given mental structure. While this structure is a unity, it functions on two levels or in two areas, the conscious and subconscious. It is the nature of the subconscious *to receive*, *to retain*, and *to act upon* whatever the conscious mind thinks and feels. It is that kind of instrument.

On the other hand, it sometimes acts in a corrective capacity. When we change our mind "on second thought," often it is our wise subconscious mind correcting the hasty decision of our conscious mind.

While the conscious mind is a law unto itself, deciding what it desires and determining its own destiny, the subconscious mind is impersonal and acts only in keeping with its own nature, that of serving the purposes of the conscious mind. Its content, its work, and its expression are determined, not by itself, but by that which is given to it to work on by the higher level of consciousness. It receives, retains and creates. Nothing which has once been given by the conscious mind to the subconscious mind to work on can be removed or expelled except by the action of the conscious mind itself.

The subconscious mind is not only a storehouse; it is an area of infinite creative activity. The purpose of this activity is to give form and expression to that which it receives from the conscious mind. It is imaginative and inventive. It never grows weary. It is the willing servant of the man or woman who understands it, and intelligently uses his or her conscious mind to direct it.

CHAPTER 5

# *The Great Submerged Area of the Subconscious*

ONE OF the greatest tragedies of the twentieth century was that of the great ocean liner *Titanic,* which sank with the loss of hundreds of lives after striking an iceberg in the North Atlantic. Such floating mountains of ice are all but submerged, usually only about one-tenth of their area showing above the surface of the water. The *Titanic* sank because it struck the mass of ice hidden below the water level.

In the total area of personality, conscious mind corresponds to the part of an iceberg that exists above the level of the water, and the subconscious mind corresponds to the many times greater part of the iceberg which lies below the level of the water.[1]

[1] *Mechanisms of Character Formation,* William A. White, Macmillan Company.

The person who expects intelligently and constructively to control his experience in life through the use of only the conscious part of his mind neglects the larger area of the subconscious. Life can be complete, purposeful, abundant and creative only if we learn how to use this submerged area.

The subconscious mind is not only the power by which great success is achieved by some; but it is likewise the channel through which failure and frustration are experienced by others. Positive and negative results depend upon the same law.

The subconscious mind brings into form and expression whatever it receives from the conscious area of mind. The content of life is determined by conscious mind—but through and by subconscious activity.

As an iceberg has little significance unless the submerged portion is considered, so the conscious aspect of our activity has limited power to achieve unless its relation to subconscious activity is properly understood and utilized.

The subconscious mind directs and sustains the vital processes and functions of life. Consider the indescribable complexity of the human body. Think of the eons of time which have been necessary for its development. Contemplate the marvelous chemical processes which begin at the moment of our conception and continue until the end of our physical life.

In pictorial terms the human body consists of some four thousand kingdoms with an aggregate population of about five hundred billion subjects. In each human body there are twelve empires of brain and nerve cells, and these alone consist of about eighty billion living individuals.[2] To the lay person these are mere "cells," but scientists know that each cell is a living individual and performs its functions more intelligently than most human beings.

These cells have body, brain and nervous systems. They respond not only to chemical stimulation, but also to mental and emotional impulses. To direct and sustain these processes and activities is obviously a task beyond the ability of the busy conscious mind.

Think of the speed, precision and balance attained in the production of blood cells. Red corpuscles are manufactured in the marrow of the long bones at the rate of about ten million every second of every minute during the life span. Quite a job, even for our subcon-

[2] *New Discoveries of Science,* **Brown Landone, Landone Foundation, Orlando, Florida.**

scious activity, to maintain this manufacturing process!

The white blood cells, on the other hand, have a super-wisdom in the presence of danger. These cells, which consume invading bacteria, multiply with terrific speed when infection enters the body. How or by whom is the order to "speed up" given?

With each advance in knowledge we gain new insight regarding these complex body processes. For example, scientific research has revealed that the size and shape of a person's body, his health and the quality of his mind, are all strangely dependent upon a group of minute structures known as the glands of internal secretion, or the endocrine glands. These small organs or glands, tucked away seemingly at random about the body, were until about forty years ago regarded as remnants of useless material left over from the workshop of creation. However, in the light of present-day science we recognize that these small organs regulate growth and health, both physical and mental.[8]

Included in this group are the adrenal glands, located directly above each kidney. These glands throw into the blood stream the solution known as adrenalin.

[8] *How We Become Personalities,* Edward H. Williams, The Bobbs-Merrill Company.

This substance is contained in the blood of a normal person in proportions of about one part adrenalin to a billion parts of arterial blood.

Another one of these glands is called the thyroid. It furnishes the blood with a secretion known as thyroxin. Human life is impossible without approximately one-hundredth of a grain of thyroxin daily.

These are but two of the simpler functions of these glands. Normal life is dependent upon their activities. How is the balance of one part of adrenalin to a billion parts of arterial blood maintained? How is the right amount of thyroxin determined each day?

One simply begs the question by saying that these and other still more complex processes are a "natural" function of the body. Back of nature, or law (chemical or otherwise), stand mind and intelligence. By all normal standards such variety and complexity require infinite mind, or intelligence. Conscious mind, of and by itself, is narrowly limited. Only that larger area of personality known as the subconscious is equal to the gigantic task of keeping the body going and meeting the varied and complex situations it must weather if it is to survive.

The dramatic power of subconscious action is perhaps best illustrated by emergency situations. The conscious mind knows that it must operate with limited power in a restricted field. The subconscious accepts no such limitation. Apparently the subconscious has potentially at its command unlimited power. This potentially unlimited power is restricted only by the assumptions of the conscious mind. In emergency situations the conscious mind is thrust aside, permitting the wisdom and power of subconscious action to express itself.

*The New York Times* recently carried the story of a man who had been confined to a hospital bed for five years, unable to move himself in any way because of complete paralysis. The hospital patient in the next bed suddenly became insane and started to attack the paralytic. The man, who for five years had been unable to move his body or walk, pulled himself loose and, without stopping, ran up three flights of stairs.

A similar story is found in an Associated Press dispatch. Eight patients, all helpless paralytics, were confined to a ward in a hospital in Ecuador. One day a giant boa constrictor visited the paralytic ward by way of an open window. In less than ten seconds the snake was the sole occupant of the ward. Every patient was suddenly and completely cured. One patient, who had not left his bed in two years, jumped from a window six feet from the ground and rapidly crossed the hospital yard. According to reliable information, each of the eight patients was completely cured of a long-standing paralytic affliction.

What gives to a lone, frail woman the strength to lift an automobile and release her husband whose life is in danger?

From what source is the soldier in battle inspired and empowered to perform amazing acts of heroism and daring?

What gave men and women the strength, during the San Francisco earthquake and fire, to perform deeds utterly impossible under normal conditions?

It is through the subconscious mind that seemingly unlimited power and strength are available in such times of emergency and danger.

* * *

During World War I the writer was stationed in a large hospital in central France. The impression of a certain patient, suffering from shock but without physical injury, remains vividly in mind. This person remained for a number of days in an upright position on his cot with his right arm extended straight out in front of his body on a level with the top of his shoulder. No support was given and nothing could induce or enable him to change the position of his arm. As every physician knows, it would be utterly impossible for a person to sustain his arm in such a position through the normal action of his mind and body for a few hours, much less several days. From what source, then, came the energy for this action? Certainly not from his conscious self.

Consider another case: The late Dr. Brown Landone was one of the great men of this generation. He was a distinguished lecturer and author, his most significant work being a seven-volume history of civilization. Although ninety-eight years old at the time of his death, his personality and general physical appearance were those of a person not over fifty, so well-preserved was he in health and physical form. He is said to have been one of the great youthful men of his generation. During his youth he was an invalid for seventeen years. His time was spent in a bed or in a wheel chair. His knees were swollen to twice the normal size and his heart was organically impaired.

One day the Landone plantation home caught fire

and this young man who could not, under any circumstances, climb a flight of stairs or walk under normal conditions, not only ran up the stairs of his home, but carried down, one after another, three heavy trunks containing valuables.

Literally hundreds of similar experiences are known to science. In the presence of danger, super-human strength is available. What is the source of this vast reserve of power? What stimulus or mental or emotional channel brings it to the surface? Such extraordinary power, such limitless and immediate wisdom must find (insofar as present-day knowledge is concerned) its source in the largely unexplored field of subconscious motivation.

CHAPTER 6

# *On Duty Twenty-Four Hours Every Day*

AS HAS already been stated, the subconscious mind is a field of unceasing activity, when we are awake or asleep. This sustained activity does much of our mental work, whether we realize it or not. Solutions to difficult problems, impossible to the limited area of the conscious mind, are found and made available. Ideas, plans, projects are generated.

A number of years ago, Dr. William Hanna Thomson, a distinguished physician and writer, recorded two very striking instances of the ability of the subconscious mind to solve problems and reach conclusions after the conscious mind had completely failed. The first of these instances was given to Dr. Thomson by a fellow student at college.

This student related that on a particular night his

roommate sat up very late in a desperate effort to solve a problem in mathematics. Notwithstanding long hours of work, he failed to find the solution. At last he rubbed his slate clean, put out the light, and went to bed. In the early hours of the morning the student was awakened by a light shining in his eyes. His roommate had turned on the light and was working at his desk. The next morning he mentioned the matter only to have his roommate deny that he had been up at any time during the night.

The first student went to the desk, picked up his roommate's slate and showed him the problem, worked out to a correct solution in his own handwriting.

This story is in no way unusual. Many people have had similar experiences.

The other incident referred to was the experience of a member of the British Diplomatic Corps in Syria. This man had been studying the Arabic language in an effort to fit himself to carry on his work among the Eastern princes and rulers. One night he attempted to compose an official letter to an Oriental ruler at Lebanon. After several hours of fruitless work he decided that the task was impossible because of his limited understanding of the language. He went to bed. One can well imagine the surprise of this man when, the following morning, he found a freshly written letter on his desk, in his own handwriting, composed in the most correct style of pure Arabic! [1]

Who solved the difficult mathematical problem? Who wrote the letter to the official in Lebanon in pure and correct Arabic? It was certainly not the conscious mind of either person. Their conscious minds had utterly failed. In these two cases, as in literally thousands of others recorded throughout the centuries from all over the world, the required skill or knowledge came out of that mysterious, unlimited, ever-active area of personality known as the subconscious.

While it is recognized on every hand that the conscious part of mind is limited, the subconscious can transcend the usual limitations of time and space. This is proved by well-attested experiences related by many people under varying conditions.

Take as an example the story of Dr. Herman V. Hilprecht, professor of the Assyrian language at the University of Pennsylvania. During the Winter of 1882–83, Dr. Hilprecht had exhausted himself trying

[1] *Brains and Personality*, William Hanna Thomson, M.D., Garden City Publishing Company.

to decipher the inscriptions on some old Assyrian rings. Finally he came to the conclusion that the task was impossible. One night he went to bed exhausted. While sleeping he dreamed. In his dream he saw a vision. A tall, stately priest of the ancient Pre-Christian Nippur Temple appeared before him and guided him to the treasure chamber of the temple. He entered a low-ceilinged room without windows where his attention was directed by the priest to a wooden chest with scraps of agate and other articles lying on the floor around it.

Clearly and distinctly the priest of the temple said, "The fragments in which you are interested and for which you have been unable to find an explanation are not finger rings. The great king, Kurigalzu, once sent to the Temple of Bel an inscribed votive cylinder of agate. At a later period, the priest of the temple suddenly received an imperative command to make at once a pair of agate earrings for the god Nippur. The priests were greatly disturbed because no new agate was at hand. In order to obey the command it was decided to cut the votive cylinder into three parts, thus making three rings. The two fragments which have caused you so much mental anguish are parts of these rings. By placing them together you will find this to be true. The third ring you will never find."

At this point Professor Hilprecht awoke and went hastily to his wife's room and told her of the dream. Then, with equal haste he went to his study. Before long the professor's wife heard him exclaim, "It is so! It is so!"

The following winter, Professor Hilprecht went to Cairo to study the objects of the Temple Nippur which had been placed in the Imperial Museum. After critical study based upon training and experience in the field of archeology, and his extended knowledge of the ancient languages, he came to the conclusion that the objects there furnished complete evidence of the correctness of his dream in every detail.[2]

* * *

The subconscious mind works creatively upon whatever is given it by the conscious mind. Its nature is set and immutable. In the conscious aspect of personality we have spontaneous choice, volition, originating action. In the subconscious, because of its nature, we have automatic reaction. The conscious mind

[2] *Human Personality and Its Survival of Bodily Death*, F. W. H. Myers, Longmans, Green & Company, Inc.

is personal, while the subconscious mind is entirely impersonal.

Every person who has ever cultivated a garden should understand the two-fold aspect of mind, and the law under which it operates. The conscious mind plants the seed in the soil. It decides what kind of seed it will plant. The soil will, by the law of its being, germinate and nourish whatever is planted—roses or potatoes.

The subconscious mind is the soil—the medium which, by its nature, contains the elements necessary for birth and growth. By the law of its being the subconscious mind will create and produce anything called for by the conscious mind. It is the nature of soil to bring forth, but it is not interested in what it brings forth. It does not know whether the plant will bear strawberries or tomatoes. The whole economy of the universe would be disturbed and destroyed should the soil not act according to its nature.

The same is true of the subconscious mind. It is a *doer*, not a *knower*. It is intelligent without knowing, and is conscious only of its purpose and nature; but it is never self-conscious.

As one of the ancient philosophers stated, the subconscious aspect of mind is a "blind force, not knowing, only doing." It is working all the time, but with most of us it works without intelligent, conscious direction. As we learn to use it consciously and constructively we shall add greatly to our control over ourselves and give greater focus and motivation to our lives. Furthermore, we shall remove much of the pressure from the conscious mind and enable it to function more easily and efficiently because it will be fresher and less confused and frustrated.

CHAPTER 7

# *Just What Do You Want from Life?*

AT THIS point suppose we make the application personal: Just what do *you* want from life?

This is undoubtedly the most important question you will ever consider. Try the plan of writing out in definite statements the things you really desire to have and to be. What will you achieve with your life: Business or professional success? A substantial income? Friends? Influence in your community? Standing in your chosen field? Fame? Power? Position? Security? Spiritual satisfactions? What?

You can, in very truth, have just about whatever you want—if you want it badly enough. But the world will give you nothing without extracting its price. By your nature, as well as by the Law of the Universe, you cannot receive or be given something for nothing.

That is not in the Scheme of Things. Take what you need and want. But pay for it you must, in one way or another.

The plain truth is this: You only really want what you are willing to pay for. If the price of attainment is too great for you to pay, you do not desire that particular thing or condition with intensity; hence you do not deserve it.

It is true that in many instances the price you must pay is unknown. Then the question becomes: are you willing to pay any price that is required? Is the thing you seek of supreme value? Is it worth more to you than any other conceivable thing or condition?

Again the answers must come from within you. The Universe is a great gambler. It seldom defines the price of anything with certainty. You must be willing to take a chance. Only one thing is certain: your desire sets the limit of your attainment. The price you are willing to pay is the measure of what you will get. You can achieve and have only that which you develop within yourself. Your ability to expand will determine what you can possess as your own. You must *be* what you *want.*

The emphasis must ever be on sustained desire. This

rules out daydreaming. Robert E. Peary had one desire—to plant the American flag at the North Pole. He tried and failed. He tried and failed again. Undaunted by difficulties and dangers that would have seemed insurmountable to a lesser soul, he tried five times before he attained his objective; but he planted the American flag on the top of the world.

Newton was asked how he made his great discoveries. "By ceaselessly thinking about them," he replied.

Little real progress is attained by indifferent, half-hearted activity or effort. Apathy, feeble emotions, or an attitude dominated by fear and doubting bring the process of personality rebuilding to a dead end.

Indeed, due to lack of sustained interest and compelling desire, and the presence of boredom, most of us ordinarily use only the top layer of our supply of energy and resources, as represented by our conscious mind. Too often the submerged area of the subconscious is left out of our plans altogether. Little wonder that so many of us only half live.

"The fault, dear Brutus," said Cassius in his famous quotation, "is not in our stars, but in ourselves, that we are underlings."

We have never become acquainted with our subconscious self; and we are short on faith to believe that there is immeasurably more knowledge and power below the surface of our personality than appears above the surface.

## CHAPTER 8

# *The Subconscious Mind as a Willing Servant*

THE idea that thoughts and feelings can be controlled, and that this power can be directed to realizing a purpose or objective chosen by the individual, is a new and strange doctrine to many people. They seem to think that mental and emotional activity come out of the dark and are applied, without purpose or reason, to the varying circumstances of life. Whatever is accomplished, or whatever goal is attained, is the result of chance or "luck."

In this belief is found the cause of the failure of so many people to achieve success and the satisfactions of life.

It is true that we have only begun to explore in any scientific way the workings of the human mind. If we know little about the conscious functioning of our mind, we know still less regarding the functioning of the subconscious. However, this does not mean that nothing is known. Investigation, research and observation have established certain methods which, if intelligently applied, will enable any individual to control his own thoughts and feelings and, through the process of this control, to accomplish much more with his life.

If a person wants to use the limitless creative power of the subconscious mind, he must learn to harness it and make it work in tandem with his conscious mind.

Before outlining the techniques for accomplishing this, it is important to stress that the subconscious is not something apart and separate from the main current of one's life. Our subconscious activity is just as much a part of our life as are our hair and eyes and arms and legs. It is not correct to say that one *has* a subconscious mind; a person *is* subconscious mind, in the same definite way that a person *is* conscious mind.

All life, regardless of the form or condition under which it expresses itself, is intelligent. We know that we are subconscious mind not because we can see or feel or measure it, but because of what our subconscious mind does.

The first step, then, in making intelligent use of the

subconscious function is to recognize in a definite conscious way that there is within us such a force as subconscious activity. That it is a part of ourselves, and that it can be controlled and directed, must be one of the basic assumptions by which we live. For the subconscious fully serves only those who believe in it.

Says Dr. Josephine A. Jackson, "We cannot see this mind, but we can see its products. To deny the subconscious is to deny the artist while looking at his picture, to disbelieve in the poet while reading his poem, and to doubt the existence of the explosive while listening to the report." [1]

If one ignores completely the fact that he has a sense of sight, the eyes are of little use. Notwithstanding the fact that the subconscious works whether it is recognized or not, it cannot be controlled and directed toward useful ends unless this recognition is present. It will give a sense of strength and permanence to know and feel that our life is not limited to the power which is available through the conscious part of our mind.

The recognition of the fact that a person's life does include subconscious mental and emotional activity

[1] From *Outwitting Our Nerves*, by Josephine A. Jackson, M.D. Used by permission of E.P. Dutton, Inc.

should also include certain fundamental facts regarding the nature of this part of a person. We must keep definitely in mind, first of all, that the subconscious is the oldest part of mind. The individual is subconscious mind long before he is conscious mind.

Every biologist knows that our five senses were developed from an "original diffused and general sensitivity" which in the very early stages must have been somewhat like the sense of touch. The subconscious mind is the development and adaptation of this mind stuff brought about by millions of years of "trial and error" experience.

From the moment of conception to the time when a baby is born, the physical organism multiplies itself by about a billion times. During this period the various organs and faculties of its mind and body are formed. The direction and control of this marvelously complex process are accomplished by the subconscious, without the aid of any conscious thought. The conscious part of the mind, which develops at birth, is simply the center of a tremendously extended field of mental and emotional activity.

The next important fact is, as already stated, that the subconscious mind is the great storehouse of life.

Every thought and every feeling we have ever experienced, our so-called instincts, the wisdom born of thousands of years of man's struggle and development, form a part of our subconscious equipment. From the standpoint of its historical development, the subconscious has within itself the limitless ability and skill which mankind has developed through many thousands of years.

Another important fact about the subconscious mind, to repeat an earlier statement, is that it will always do what it is told to do—if it is told in the right way. By the law of its being it can do nothing else. Once we master the art of directing our subconscious mind, it becomes a willing and completely dependable servant.

CHAPTER 9

# *The Knack of Using the Subconscious Mind*

IF THE subconscious is to be the servant of the conscious mind, it is important to know how it can be reached and by what method direction and information can be given to it. It is only in the conscious part of the mind that the power of choice or the ability to select is found. Furthermore, since the subconscious mind does not discriminate, does not decide what is good and what is bad, its selecting and deciding must be done for it by the conscious mind. It is not intelligent in the sense that it can select or reject what is given to it, so it must be directed with care.

So much for the conditions under which the subconscious will serve us. Now for the techniques which make up the "knack."

The subconscious is reached, first of all, by what we

generally term "autosuggestion." By this term only one thing is meant: talking to one's self. Since the subconscious is a part of the person, the person is certainly talking to himself when he talks to the subconscious.

However, keep in mind that in order for our thoughts to influence our subconscious mind they must have purpose, emotional power and definiteness.

Our subconscious mind will believe anything and everything we say to it.

That is why the statement made popular by the great French psychiatrist, Coué, "Every day in every way I am getting better and better," was sound psychology. The all-inclusive thought that life progresses, enhanced in meaning and value, when directed repeatedly to the subconscious, will convince that area of the mind that the statement is *true;* and what is more important, that the statement embodies what the conscious mind really *wants to be true.*

When told this, the subconscious mind applies all its power toward creating a more wholesome, efficient type of living, drawing on its stored knowledge and experience. Every day in every way one actually *becomes* better and better!

That this method, as used by Coué, did actually

cure thousands of seriously sick people was a fact. That it improved the lives of other thousands who were not sick, but who wanted to live still happier and healthier lives, is equally true.

A reference to the phenomenon of hypnosis may help in understanding the role of autosuggestion in controlling subconscious activity. A great deal of intelligent research is being done in this field, which has nothing whatever in common with the parlor entertainment or medicine show brand of hypnotism. In hypnosis the thing that happens seems to be this: As the result of suggestion on the part of the operator, and susceptibility (or acceptance) on the part of the subject, the latter's conscious mind steps aside, its function and activity temporarily suspended, and a direct channel to the subconscious is opened. In this state, suggestions and directions can be planted directly in the subconscious area.

Consider the following experience reported by the *British Medical Journal* in a recent issue: Since birth the skin below the neck of a 16-year-old boy had been as hard and crusty as fish scales. Every skill known to medical science had been applied without results. As a last resort, the boy was hypnotized and told that the condition on his left arm would presently disappear.

Five days later the horny area on the arm peeled off and the skin became soft and pink. Subsequent hypnotic suggestions cleared the scales from most of his arm and leg surfaces. What strange subconscious powers brought about this cure, a cure admittedly beyond the skill of medical science?

The glib assumption by many people that autosuggestion is simply a method of fooling one's self is not supported by realistic, scientific study. The truly scientific mind accepts a fact whether or not it knows how or why it came to be a fact. It is not greatly important that we do not know just how or why an assumption of well-being, of good health, or of success will influence the subconscious mind and start its creative power working to bring about these conditions. That it does so work, and that definite and specific results are achieved, is not open to question; it has been demonstrated in many thousands of lives.

However, it is not assumed that every person can or will apply this method with equal success; and certainly the process requires faith and perseverance. It is of little value to direct an affirmative idea of well-being to the subconscious and at the same time cross our fingers in recognition of the fact that we do not believe what we are saying. Sincerity, scientific impartiality, along with something like the unspoiled faith of a child, are necessary. And one must not be discouraged if results are not immediately apparent.

Many, if not most, of us have used our subconscious mind so little, in the sense of giving it orders, that it is a rusty instrument. But, just as a rusty machine will respond to lubrication and use, so the subconscious mind will gain steadily in flexibility and dependability when lubricated with faith and used with persistence.

* * *

As brought out in the opening chapter, relaxation is the key by which the door to the subconscious is opened. For some strange reason, intense mental activity prevents or delays the work of the subconscious mind. This is not to say, however, that sustained conscious mental activity is unnecessary before a problem or an order is turned over to the subconscious.

One writer [1] has likened the process of gearing the conscious and subconscious areas of the mind for ef-

[1] Robert R. Updegraff, *The Subconscious Mind in Business* (out of print). Also articles in *Forbes,* September 15, 1948 and *The Reader's Digest,* October, 1948.

fective subconscious thinking to the process of "fireless cooking." Some modern ranges have ovens with insulated walls which store heat when the gas or electricity is on and release it slowly long after the oven burner has been turned off. Carrying out the cooking analogy, this writer likens the conscious mind to the burner which starts the cooking process, and the subconscious mind to the insulated oven in which the cooking is finished on stored heat.

This is an apt analogy, and effectively illustrates the technique of using the subconscious mind.

To do all our mental "cooking" with our conscious mind is to burn mental and emotional energy wastefully and at tremendously high cost to our nervous system. Whereas, to use our subconscious mind to do the "cooking" with retained heat is to use our past experience, our mental energy and our time with the greatest possible efficiency. For while a problem or an idea is "cooking" it draws upon all our stored knowledge, experience and understanding.

When we give an assignment to the subconscious mind in the form of a definite problem or question or commission, we start the "cooking." At this stage the conscious mind should focus on it, accumulating the necessary facts, ideas, information and relevant data for the subconscious mind to work on. The conscious mind must be focused on the material long enough and intently enough to get it thoroughly heated. Then, and not until then, should it be turned over to the subconscious mind.

The author referred to, who has many major problems to cope with in connection with several businesses, has gone so far as to have blanks printed to use for organizing his problems for "fireless cooking." A copy of one of these blanks, filled out with a typical problem, is reproduced on the following page.

Under "Statement of the Problem" he boils down to a sentence or two just what the problem is, stated simply and baldly. This "turns on the heat." In the next space he sets down *five* possible approaches to the problem. This helps to engage his subconscious mind and starts the "cooking." In the third space he jots down any ideas he has thought of, "up to now," whether or not they are particularly sensible or appropriate. He knows that solutions to problems frequently come from the most unexpected directions.

He stresses the fact that in filling out this "cooker" sheet he does not try to *answer* any of the questions.

## SUBCONSCIOUS "COOKER" SHEET

**Date** *June 12* **Bring Up** *Every Monday A.M.*

**Statement of the Problem:**

*Jim Blake is proving a failure as a department head. We must salvage him or fire him.*

**FIVE Possible Approaches to a Solution:**

1. *Put him on notice that he has only four months to come through.*
2. *He has a fine wife. Can we get her help?*
3. *Ask my associates if they have any ideas for saving him.*
4. *Try praising him.*
5. *Go fishing with him.*

**These are my thoughts up to now:**

*He was promoted because he seemed to have all necessary qualifications for the job. What has happened to him — or has the job changed?*

*He seems to have grown lazy. Maybe we haven't found the way to fire his interest. Or is there something wrong with him physically?*

*What does he appear to like about the job?*

*What does he appear to dislike?*

*What parts of his job does he do well?*

*How would I handle his job if I had it?*

He leaves them for his subconscious mind to work on.

In the upper right-hand corner he "tickles" the sheet to be brought up for "stirring." If no solution has come to him meanwhile, on the date it comes up for review he reads over what he had written; then, in the bottom space, he adds any new thoughts that come to him as he reviews the problem.

Sometimes, he reports, going over this sheet the first or second time "taps" his subconscious and produces a solution. But if it does not, he does not worry. He has given the problem a good "stirring." He relegates it to his subconscious mind once more and goes about his business.

Sooner or later—it may be a matter of hours or days or weeks—this process nearly always produces the solution, with no wear and tear on his conscious mind.

He uses these sheets not only to solve his problems, but to work out constructive plans for the future.

Any one of us can accomplish the same result simply by crystallizing a problem that is facing us in a sentence or two and jotting it down on a slip of paper, then adding brief notes of all the possible ideas or solutions our conscious mind can think of at that particular moment. Our subconscious will then take over.

If you keep the paper on which you have made your "cooking" notes, the next morning—or whenever you take up the subject again—as you glance at your notes you may suddenly see the solution to your problem. Your subconscious had it ready for you and needed only to be jogged.

Sometimes, in starting the "fireless cooking," instead of writing out your problem on paper it may be better to talk it out with some associate or friend, or a member of your family. Indeed, some people may use this method entirely because they can talk things out better than they can write; talking is their method of thinking. It makes no difference how you crystallize your problem, so long as you get it organized for your subconscious mind to work on.

At this point an important fact should be brought out: because the subconscious mind is not rational, but draws on our intuitive faculties and approaches every problem without relation to tradition or logic, we may not at first recognize the idea or solution it presents as being the help we are looking for. It is necessary, if we are to take our subconscious into partnership, to train ourselves to be open-minded, and to keep asking ourselves: Is it possible that this strange idea that has popped into my mind is the solution I have been seeking?

*   *   *

Many people's conscious minds are "one track"; they can concentrate on just one thing at a time. Fortunately for all of us, any number of problems can be turned over to the subconscious mind, where they will all "cook" at the same time, without the least confusion.

Usually the "fireless-cooking" process cannot be hurried; the subconscious can seldom be lashed into action. Then again, under certain conditions it works with surprising speed.

Sometimes it acts explosively—an idea or the solution to a problem blows off the lid, as it were, and pops out. At other times an idea or plan, or the answer to some intricate problem, unfolds like the petals of a flower. Once in a while the operation resembles the putting together of a picture-puzzle. Today the subconscious supplies one piece, tomorrow one or two more, and so on, until suddenly some morning the picture is complete.

Meanwhile, once the subconscious has been given an assignment, the conscious mind can be turned to other matters, with no further immediate concern about the problem in question. The farther afield it goes, the better. Best of all, seek complete mental relaxation by turning to some activity which you especially enjoy. Play golf, read a detective story, lunch or dine well and leisurely, go to a concert or the movies, play bridge or canasta, take a brisk walk, or do something that requires skill of hand. Consciously tune out the conscious mind, as you would turn off a radio or television program. Let it go on a vacation!

Sometimes while the "cooking" process is going on, little segments of a solution of a problem will flash into the conscious mind. It is well to stop and think about them for a few minutes. The subconscious mind may be ready to report. On the other hand, it may be merely the steam from the process of subconscious cerebration penetrating the conscious mind, much as the aroma of the turkey roasting in the oven penetrates the house on Thanksgiving day with its enticing promise. We should not ignore this symptom of progress; neither need we force it unless we are under pressure of time. But it is always encouraging.

Learning to use the subconscious mind—consciously—is like forming any new habit. In forming a new habit, you have to repeat it until it becomes automatic.

In learning this new habit of using your subconscious mind, you will have to discard your old habit—of straining to solve problems with your conscious mind. You must use your conscious mind to *start* the "fireless cooking." But you must then accustom yourself to letting your subconscious mind take over.

Another point to bear in mind in forming the new habit is that your subconscious mind can be trained on the many little problems that make up your working day, as well as your life at home. Once you learn the "knack" of "fireless cooking" your little problems, the bigger and tougher ones will take care of themselves in the same easy fashion. Then your new habit will really begin to pay off!

CHAPTER 10

# "In Leisure There Is Luck"

ONE man to whom the writer was describing the art of using the subconscious mind remarked, "That's all right for anybody who wants to make a sweatshop of his mind. I don't."

This man had missed the point completely. It is true that it is sometimes necessary to explore an idea or problem consciously to the point of mental fatigue. But who of us does not from time to time work to the point of exhaustion of both mind and body? The whole purpose of learning to use our subconscious mind is to give our conscious mind more time to rest, while our subconscious works for us tirelessly, without thought or effort on our part.

As a matter of fact, subconscious activity requires time and thrives on relaxation and a sense of leisure.

Perhaps that is what the late Andrew Mellon had in mind when he said, "In leisure there is luck."

It would be impossible to overemphasize the importance, once the "cooking" has been well started, of turning to something pleasurable and relaxing, something that produces a sense of ease and well-being. For such a mood produces a feeling of confidence. And confidence is important to success in using the subconscious mind.

Recall the statement by the German physicist von Helmholtz in the opening chapter, that "happy ideas never came to me when my mind was fatigued or when I was at my working table."

* * *

A well-known novelist makes this interesting observation in one of his books: [1]

"I get my best ideas for writing when I'm farming, and my best farm ideas when writing. Milking cows is very fine for ironing out plot difficulties. There is something soothing and stimulating to the mental processes in that rhythmic tug and squeeze, the quiet physical rote movement of it, the cow's warm flank,

[1] From *Green Mountain Farm,* by Elliott Merrick, copyright 1948. Used by permission of the author.

the smell of hay, the white streams building up in the pail. . . . A sense of being a peasant—clod-like and one with the earth—comes to me. I do not think, I am not required to think, there is no necessity to think. All conscious effort, all self-consciousness, and all the natural blocks are gone. Consequently I sit there teeming with story stuff. It flows through me as though I were a stranger and bystander, amused, non-recording, not concerned. I can't wait to get to a desk where I can set it all down. But after a little while at the desk I get thinking about cows again, and how will I get another, and how can I raise the money to seed some more fields in order to keep her in the manner to which she is accustomed."

* * *

The following paragraph describes the way Metternich, the great Austrian statesman, used—and implicitly depended upon—his subconscious mind; and the efficacy of the leisurely confident approach:

"It is interesting to note the way in which his (Metternich's) mind worked in solving a problem. 'The necessary results mature rapidly,' he said, 'under apparent distractions. While eating, in ordinary conversation or in riding, the clearest revelations and the most important ideas come. As soon as the object has ripened quite lucidly within me and my mind and spirit are saturated with it, I put it upon paper, unworried about order and sequence, which then arrange themselves of their own accord.' His private physician, Dr. Jaeger, tells that Metternich had just returned from a wearisome night journey when he was met by a courier with an important dispatch. The courier asked what the answer was to be. Metternich replied: 'I really do not know yet. Let me first finish the novel in my travel-bag. Perhaps the answer will come.' "[2]

One businessman who uses the "fireless-cooking" technique on practically all of his problems, uses his golf game as a regular part of his working technique. The following paragraph from one of this man's letters is a short course in combining golf and business:

"I've learned how to make a golf game pay for the time it takes. Instead of letting myself work up to the hour when I'm to leave for the links without any thought of what I want the afternoon's mental relaxation to do for me, I make it a point, before leaving my

[2] From *Metternich*, by Arthur Herman. Used by special permission of E.P. Dutton, Inc.

office, to dig into some problem just far enough to get the elements lined up clearly in my mind or on paper. Then I put them out of my conscious thought—shove them back into the subconscious—and forget them while I play golf. As a matter of fact, one simply can't think consciously about business problems out on the links. (I know because I've tried.) The problem simmers away. Sometimes it's all 'cooked' into a solution by the time I'm back in my street clothes; sometimes it isn't. But I've noticed that following an afternoon of golf, the solution is nearly always ready by the time I reach my desk the next morning, and I know my afternoon wasn't wasted. Since I've learned this 'fireless cooking' technique I always think of my country club as my eighteen-hole office. . . . The trick is in focusing on the problem for half an hour or so before you leave the office, and cutting it up into small pieces for easier 'cooking.' "

Another successful executive who declares he has developed the use of his subconscious mind so that it does about two-thirds of his work says, "I find that I no longer approach impossible problems as being impossible, but merely as problems requiring long, slow cooking, like the tougher cuts of meat."

A stern word of caution is in order at this point: one dare not make the mistake of assuming that the subconscious mind will do *all* of one's work; or that it will do *any* of it without concentration on the matter by the conscious mind. What is more, the ingredients of the dish to be "cooked" whether it is a problem requiring solution, a difficulty to be surmounted, a troublesome letter to be answered, a way to handle some ticklish situation, a name for a new product, have to be assembled and mixed into a sort of mental batter.

Only then, can the subconscious be expected to take over. And it may be necessary to turn on the direct heat from time to time, that is, do a bit of conscious thinking to keep the problem "cooking."

Eventually the subconscious mind will nearly always deliver. And its finished product will usually be superior to that of the conscious mind. For the subconscious is wiser. It has the accumulated experience of the years—if not the centuries—to draw upon.

* * *

A professional man who has consciously cultivated his subconscious mind over a period of years says that he not only uses the working-consciously-until-fatigued method in attacking major projects; but he employs a modification of this technique in the daily routine of his professional activities. Whenever he is working at any task and strikes a snag, or finds himself in a blind alley, he lays the task aside and turns to something else for a time.

"Often," he reports, "in an hour or so—and sometimes in a matter of minutes—my subconscious comes to my rescue by revealing the next step. Then I tackle the job again and work at it until I strike another snag, whereupon I let my subconscious take over again."

In this way this man accomplishes much with a surprisingly small investment of time, and—even more important—outwits his frustrations.

This was the method employed by Dr. Charles W. Eliot, long-time president of Harvard, who gave as an explanation of why he was able to accomplish so much, that whenever he found his way blocked in one project or enterprise, he turned to another where progress was possible.

Part of his secret was that he allowed time for events to catch up; for often the time is not ripe, in the Scheme of Things, for progress along a given path. But an important factor in Dr. Eliot's technique was that his subconscious mind took over and helped unblock his path by supplying him with fresh ideas for the solution to his problems.

* * *

Henry David Thoreau was a dreamer, but, like so many dreamers, he had some exceedingly practical thoughts. Following is a pertinent paragraph from his *Journal:*

"The really efficient laborer will be found not to crowd his day with work, but will saunter to his tasks surrounded by a wide halo of ease and leisure. There will be a wide margin for relaxation to his day. He is only earnest to secure the kernels of time, and does not exaggerate the value of the husk. Why should the hen set all day? She can lay but one egg, and besides she will not have picked up materials for a new one. Those who work much do not work hard."

The extremely busy, overworked person will benefit little from the services of his subconscious mind unless or until he slows down and gives it a chance.

It is necessary to cultivate not only faith but patience and a sense of leisure if one is really to master the use of the subconscious. Andrew Mellon was right: "In leisure there is luck."

## CHAPTER II

# *The Subconscious Mind in Business*

WHEN a man takes a position with a business in an executive or administrative capacity, the enterprise that employs him is entitled to the services of both parts of his mind, but in far too many cases it gets the benefit of only one. The conscious mind goes on the payroll as a matter of course, but the subconscious mind, which as a rule does far better work, is allowed to loaf.

Manifestly, this is unfair to the business; and it is just as unfair to the man—and to his wife and children, if he has a family. He is hiring out his shallow surface mind and letting the rich depths of his subconscious mind slumber while time hastens him toward the end of his usefulness.

There is need in business for much concentrated

conscious cerebration. There is need, often, for intense application, sometimes over long periods. There are even times for rushing.

But there are also times to relax and let the subconscious mind do its part of the work. It is accomplishment that we are after, not more activity. Accomplishment knows no office hours. Progress has little to do with desks or office routine.

A quaint story told by Herbert Quick demonstrates the value of taking time to let things "cook." This story concerns the great-grandfather of Diedrich Knickerbocker. On taking the contract to build a church in Rotterdam, the old gentleman took three months of smoking for pure consideration of the work; then three more in visiting every church on a circuitous journey from Rotterdam through Amsterdam, Delft, Haarlem, Leyden, and The Hague and back to Rotterdam; then three more in walking and navigating and climbing to attain coigns of vantage for contemplating the site of the still unbuilt church.

At last, having smoked three hundredweight of tobacco, and traveled and thought and contemplated for full twelve months, and having filled the good Rotterdammers with the fidgets, he pulled off his coat and five pairs of breeches and laid the corner-stone of the church. According to the great historian of New Amsterdam, when the church was completed "all the zealous Christians of Rotterdam preferred it to any other."

* * *

The businessman who takes many hours to mature his plans, and comparatively few to carry them out, as did old Knickerbocker in taking twelve months to perfect a mental blueprint of his church before taking his trowel in hand to lay the cornerstone, will come out fully as well. It is the accomplishment philosophy as contrasted with the activity fetish.

If the head of a business, or a department of a business, will take an hour off occasionally and jot down on a sheet of paper the problems he can see looming in the weeks or months ahead—special projects to be undertaken, unpleasant actions that are almost certain to have to be taken, difficult decisions that are going to have to be made—he will be starting the "cooking," thus using his subconscious mind intelligently.

If a person were to work on this basis two or three weeks—or even several months—ahead in connection with major plans and problems, and at least twenty-four hours ahead in meeting his routine responsibilities, he would just about *double* his effectiveness as a worker.

Our great trouble is that we do not make a *start* on our difficult or unpleasant jobs; we keep waiting until we can see just how to handle them. The longer we wait the more difficult, not to say impossible, they appear. If we would only engage our conscious minds briefly—turn on the heat and *start* the "cooking"—our subconscious minds would take over much of the load.

* * *

This way of working relegates an office to its rightful place in the scheme of operations of any executive with the responsibility for formulating policies, developing ideas, and motivating those who must carry on the detailed work of running a business.

Actually, the only purpose of an office is to serve as a directing center and contact point for putting into effect the ideas and plans and decisions arrived at in one's mind, consciously or subconsciously, during the twenty-four hours of the day.

As for desks, they are not thinking machines; in fact they, with the papers that clutter them, are apt to be distractions rather than helps to thinking. They are the one place where a man gets so close to his problems that he can get little perspective on them.

Desk-bound thinking is probably more responsible than is the lack of business acumen for many poor plans and decisions. Certainly it is responsible for the lack of progress in many businesses, and for the paucity of fresh ideas and new conceptions.

One reason the late Henry Ford was able to evolve so many original and revolutionary policies was that he seldom used a desk. His thinking was done on his feet, wherever he happened to be.

Such desk-free thinking is likely to be sounder thinking because it gives the subconscious mind a better opportunity to operate; ordinarily, too, it is less of a strain on the conscious mind, for it is less concentrated and the thinker is subject to less mental irritation from the interruptions of office routine.

Perhaps businesses would be more soundly administered, if, like Ford, their top officials had no regular place to sit down. At least they would break up the habit of harnessing the conscious mind to a desk for eight hours of the day and denying the subconscious partner equal opportunity to function.

The subconscious can help in the day's routine in many little ways. For example, the late Lord Leverhulme, one of England's great industrial geniuses, had a dictation technique which commends itself to any executive with a volume of correspondence.

Starting with a pile of letters, Leverhulme would dictate until he came to some letter which he could not readily answer. Instead of stopping to struggle with it, he would shift it to the bottom of the pile. Continuing with the next letter, he would go on until he encountered another difficult letter, which he would also transfer to the bottom.

By the time he had reached the bottom of the original pile, his subconscious mind had usually worked out the answer to the first tough letter. If not, he again shifted it to the bottom, and tackled the next, or the next. In the end, he might be left with one or two really difficult letters, which he would either struggle with until he had mastered, or lay aside to "cook" a day or two longer.

The head of a New York advertising agency, whose stock in trade is creating ideas, has found that he can use what he calls his "time margins" to engage his subconscious mind in new problems. Between appointments, or while waiting for a telephone connection, this man jots down on a scratch pad the salient facts, or such stray thoughts as he may have about the problem. This, he finds, is sufficient to start the fireless-cooking process. Some of his best ideas have come to him as a result of these hastily scribbled notes.

* * *

One businessman whose conventional office is in a New York skyscraper, says his real office is a mile of sidewalk. That mile of sidewalk extends from his home to the suburban station from which he commutes. He always walks to the station in the morning, and as he walks his mind leisurely arranges the matters to which he wishes to give attention that day, with the result that when he arrives at the office, after a thirty-minute ride on the train during which he has an opportunity to read the morning newspaper and get a focus on the news of the world, the major projects for the day are sharply outlined in his mind. No matter how many interruptions he may encounter, those major projects stand out clearly in his mind all day and he works them out between interruptions.

Were he to arrive at the office without this definite plan in his mind, he would promptly get caught in the office routine and the day would be spent before he could even visualize what that day ought to have shown in the way of accomplishment and progress.

This man uses his mile-long office again at night for reviewing the day, mentally noting what he was able to accomplish, and marshaling the problems of the morrow for his subconscious mind to work on during the night. Arriving at his front door, he drops all thought of business and lives a normal and relaxed life with his family.

In the morning when he again starts out on his mile-walk he has the benefit of overnight "cooking" of the major problems confronting him, and their solutions often emerge and fit right into his thinking for the new day, without his having had to give them a moment's conscious concern.

* * *

Different individuals must, of course, follow different methods; but does it not seem reasonable for every man to determine how and where he does his best thinking, and so to arrange his day, and if need be to rearrange his living habits with this in mind? Find a man who can accomplish the seemingly impossible in spite of everything and you find a man who can boss himself as well as others, and who has developed the ability to ignore the nonessentials and drive for a result, even if he has to turn his days upside down to achieve it.

Complete relaxation is one businessman's key to the door of the subconscious mind. This man's doctor had told him that he simply had to relax more. Not being able to get away from his office until the closing hour, he has acquired the habit of dropping into an easy chair in the corner of his office for fifteen minutes three or four times a day and picking up a book of fiction or biography from the table beside this chair and forgetting all of his business concerns.

He has found that he has to keep a memo pad and a lead pencil on the table beside him because so many ideas come popping into his mind while he is reading that he would have to get up every few minutes and go over to his desk to make notes if this pad were not handy. He never sits down in his easy chair with any conscious thought of developing ideas, but he finds that in a very few minutes his conscious mind becomes completely relaxed and his subconscious mind begins to deliver ideas.

This executive stumbled upon his particular solution of the problem of getting his subconscious mind geared into his business thinking. The discovery was accidental but he now uses it by design.

The executive vice-president of a large corporation to whom the author had explained the mechanics of using the subconscious mind wrote, "I tried out my subconscious mind last night on one of the tough problems I was telling you about, but I am sorry to say it didn't come through with a solution this morning. I guess I'm not gifted with subconscious cerebration."

Here was a man who had been struggling with a problem in his conscious mind for many months without success; yet he expected his subconscious mind to solve it overnight. The subconscious seldom works that fast. In solving a really tough problem, two things are necessary: time and repeated "stirring." Then, one day, when the problem is farthest from one's thoughts, a solution is likely to begin to filter through into the conscious mind. Or else to come in a flash, and cause one to say, "Why didn't I think of *that* before?"

The executive mentioned above should have started with minor problems until he had *formed the habit* of using his subconscious mind. Then, in time, his tougher problems would resolve themselves naturally.

CHAPTER 12

# *The Art of Balancing the Mind-Load*

THE only criticism the writer has encountered to the idea of making conscious use of the subconscious mind in the solution of business problems came from a keen businessman (who, incidentally, is a past-master at balancing his mental work-load between his conscious and subconscious, though he does not realize it) who argued that the whole idea is reactionary.

"It is a throwback to intuition and hunches," he objected, "whereas we are trying to develop a science of business, with hunches and all that sort of thing thrown into the discard. Is not all the work of our graduate business schools nullified by this scheme for junking logic and rationalization?"

As a matter of fact, there is no thought of junking

logic or rationalization as a working method, or of relaxing the effort to develop a science of business.

Research and rationalization, leading to scientifically determined facts and principles, are becoming increasingly important factors in business administration. They are effective aids to the conscious part of our work, for they are useful in starting the mental "cooking." They are, in fact, the fuel; without them we can hardly make a fire hot enough to carry the conscious mental "cooking" to the point where problems can safely be left to the subconscious mind.

The trouble with business in the past has been that it has played intuition and hunches without a sound foundation of information, properly organized. The graduate business school's mission is to teach young men how to prepare fact-foundations and principle-foundations for their thinking. If these schools insist on rationalization as the sole method, then we may break with them. For purely rationalized decisions are frequently dangerous because they are very likely to leave out some important consideration that comes out of a man's innate common sense. Or they forego the benefit of age-old instinct or mental inheritance which will be supplied by his subconscious if he gives it a chance to help out. But there is no evidence of such insistence on the part of business educators; they seem to be trying to teach us to work with facts rather than unsupported opinions, and to use our minds to the best possible advantage.

Some day, it is the writer's strong conviction, business schools will provide a course in the art of balancing the mental load, which will in reality be a course in the use of the subconscious mind. No more valuable start could be given a young man than to train him how to balance his mind-load and bring all of his powers to bear on every problem that confronts him.

CHAPTER 13

# *A Fortune from a Hobby*

IT WILL bear repeating yet again: the wonderful thing about the subconscious mind is that it works best when we are doing what we like best to do —when we are following some hobby, whether it be whittling, listening to a symphony concert, painting pictures, writing verse, tinkering with an automobile, climbing a mountain, gardening, playing tennis, sailing a boat, or what-not. In short, when it is taking a temporary vacation.

A happy mind is a healthy mind, and a healthy mind, like a healthy body, puts drive back of a man's mental activity. It was Andrew Carnegie, that shrewd old Scot, who knew how to conserve his mental vitality as well as his money, who wrote, "My young partners do the work and I do the laughing, and I recommend to you the thought that there is little success where there is little laughing."

Many of the great discoveries were made by men when they were following a hobby, rather than their vocation. For years the author has cherished a yellowed clipping, cut from a magazine long since defunct, which raises the thought that there may be a fortune in a hobby: "The father of photography was an army officer; and of the electric motor, a bookbinder's clerk. The inventor of the telegraph was a portrait painter; and of the jacquard loom, a dressmaker. A farmer invented the typewriter; a poet, the sewing machine; a cabinet-maker, the cotton gin; and a coal miner, the locomotive. The telephone was the after-school work of a teacher of the deaf; the disc talking machine, the night work of a clothing salesman; the wax cylinder phonograph, of a lawyer's clerk; the typesetting machine, a groceryman. A physician made the first pneumatic tire because his little son was an invalid. The story of nearly every great invention has been the result of some one riding a hobby."

None of us may have the luck to develop a fortune-making invention in our leisure time; but having a consuming hobby may contribute greatly to our good fortune if we learn to use it as a period for resting our conscious mind and letting the subconscious bring out the best there is in us—of ideas, plans, solutions to problems.

CHAPTER 14

# Our Subconscious Potential

MEN and women of only average education and ability can achieve marked success, and rise to positions of prominence and influence, by mastering the art of drawing upon their subconscious potential. Some of the great discoveries of science have been made by people of no special skill or reputation.

For example, one night in October, 1920, in Toronto, Canada, Frederick Grant Banting, a young surgeon with so little professional practice that he had to teach in order to make a living, was working over his lecture for the following day. The disease on which he was working was diabetes, the dreaded affliction of millions of people, for which at that time medical science could offer no means of control.

Hour after hour Banting studied the literature of

this disease. His mind was a confused maze of conflicting theories, case histories and accounts of experiments with dogs. At a late hour he went wearily to bed. At two o'clock in the morning he suddenly woke up. His subconscious mind had something to report!

Getting up, he turned on a light and wrote three short sentences in his note book: "Tie off pancreatic duct of dogs. Wait six to eight weeks for degeneration. Remove residue and extract." Turning off the light, he went back to bed and to sleep.

It was those three sentences which led to the discovery of insulin. Banting's conscious mind had come to grips with one of the baffling problems in medical science, but could find no solution. His subconscious mind finished the job and thus gave life and hope to millions of afflicted persons.

Note that Banting had been mentally struggling with the problem of diabetes; that his mind was a confused maze of theories, case histories, and accounts of experiments. In other words, the "cooking" had been well started by his conscious mind.

* * *

The solution of many a major problem in our business, professional or personal lives will be supplied by our subconscious minds if we do a sufficiently good job of "pre-cooking."

Some years ago fourteen hundred and fifty outstanding research chemists were surveyed to find how and when new ideas came to them.[1] This group represented the leading research laboratories as well as the large chemical manufacturing industries of the land. The work of these men accounted for the major advances of the chemical industry made during the previous twenty-five years.

The questionnaire asked these eminent scientists to describe how and when significant new ideas and insights arrived. Did they come while they were actively studying data related to their unsolved problem? Was the solution to the problem found in the laboratory during office hours? Did the required wisdom result from a process of careful, conscious reasoning, or did it arrive as a sudden flash, a "hunch," a full-grown concept from the subconscious level of mind?

Practically all these men replied that solutions rarely came while working in the laboratory or while

[1] Washington Platt and Ross A. Baker in *Journal of Chemical Education,* Volume 8, Number 10, pp. 1969–2002.

engrossed in the study of data. Their great discoveries came in moments of relaxation following intensive application. Their great insights did not arrive as the result of cold logic and reasoning, but sprang into consciousness, full and complete, at odd moments in strange places.

One stated that the idea for a great advance came when, "freeing my mind of all thought of the problem, I walked briskly down Tremont Street when . . . as if from the clear sky above me, an idea popped into my head suddenly." For another the needed insight arrived, "while riding on a train." Another scientist found the solution to his problem while "sitting at my desk doing nothing and thinking of other matters."

According to these scientists, ideas occur in most unorthodox fashion. One had an idea that resulted in a significant change in a manufacturing process, "while dodging automobiles across Park Row and Broadway." Another found the solution to his problem, "while dressing after bathing in the sea."

Other members of the group made discoveries and solved problems in many diverse ways and at unexpected times: "In the bed at three o'clock in the morning." "Sunday morning in church while the preacher was announcing his text." To others, new ideas came while shaving and dressing, when gardening, fishing, playing solitaire, and while walking between their homes and offices.

In general discoveries were made following full investigation of the problem, exhaustive study of all available data—then change and relaxation. These modern researchers have a close spiritual kinship with Archimedes who solved the problem of specific gravity while having his morning bath.

* * *

Before any major problem is given to the subconscious to work on, the matter should be studied and investigated in all its aspects. The known facts and available figures should be assembled. All data from every angle should be examined until it is understood. The arguments for and against any particular solution should be worked out in detail. After all the facts are gathered, the problem or question should be stated in specific terms, preferably on paper. In a word, the subconscious mind should be given a *specification.* But this caution should be observed: the specification should involve the *result,* not the *method.* Often the subconscious mind attacks a problem from an oblique angle and we do not realize at the time that it has solved it. We are so used to thinking on the basis of conventional solutions that we often overlook what seems unpromising, perhaps even foolish—but may turn out to be the obvious solution! And it is the obvious that we are forever overlooking.

* * *

The subconscious can nearly always be depended upon for results if the assignment is *definite*, and if it is given power by calm, purposeful *desire*. The French psychologist, Theodule Ribot, observed wisely that the inventive process—and the subconscious is creatively inventive—springs from desire, which arouses images that the imagination arranges and combines.

The answer may come during one's awakening moments, or it may arrive unannounced at any time of the day.

Descartes, the French mathematician and philosopher, is said to have made his great discoveries while lying in bed in the morning. As previously stated, many men have discovered that they get their best ideas while shaving. This is not strange. While their conscious function has been at rest during the night their subconscious has been busy, and this is its first chance to report on its night's work.

Not that the subconscious mind will always deliver an idea or produce a solution overnight. It may require days, or even weeks or months. It may be necessary, in connection with major problems, for the conscious mind to re-examine the problem and turn it back to the subconscious for study time after time. This is why it is wise to start the "cooking" as far ahead as possible. The subconscious will then be allowed time for its work, and the conscious mind has the comforting knowledge that the problem is in process of solution.

It is not enough to believe in the existence, power and wisdom of the subconscious mind. To secure results, a person must have living faith in the final outcome. He must be convinced in his heart that there is an answer to the question his mind is asking. He must be confident that there is a solution—a right solution to the problem. Further, he must be confident that the right solution will come to him at the right time.

It is at this point that many people fail, and for this reason: The subconscious will not accept a thing as true unless the conscious mind itself actually believes that it is true. And the subconscious mind cannot find a solution unless the conscious mind honestly believes that a solution is possible. So faith is an important ingredient in the formula.

The conscious mind does not know what the solution will be, or how it is to be found. That is not necessary; but it must have faith that a solution is possible. The solutions to some problems are utterly irrational and illogical. That is why the conscious mind cannot arrive at them. They may violate all known rules, reverse every reasonable concept, fly in the face of experience—yet be the solutions. Perhaps brilliant ones!

Genius knows no limitations of logic, rules or previous experience. Perhaps all of us could develop some of the attributes of genius if we would resolutely refuse to be limited by our sensible, logical, conservative conscious mind, and turned to our inventive-creative subconscious mind whenever we face a difficult problem.

And right here the point may well be stressed again that the subconscious is not limited to the solution of problems. If we look around us at the world's needs, at the possibilities in our business or profession, and at the opportunities to do new things in new ways, we will discover unlimited scope for the creative use of the subconscious.

The world moves forward in surges as here a man and there a woman makes a fresh and daring discovery, or proposes some bold new idea. If the truth were known, most of such contributions to progress probably come from the subconscious mind of some person who has broken the bounds of conventional, conscious thinking.

Said Thomas Edison, who himself contributed so much to progress, "The key to successful methods comes right out of the air. A real, new thing like a general idea, a beautiful melody, is pulled out of space."

Space in this sense represents the area of the subconscious.

There is literally no limit to the creative potential of this amazing yet little used area of the mind of every one of us!

CHAPTER 15

# *In Tune with Infinite Mind*

MIND itself is not complete; it relates to some power or force outside of itself, on which it draws, consciously or unconsciously. What is this power or force?

In attempting to build a philosophy of life and achievement, reason and experience alike require the assumption of a First Cause—an Infinite Mind. We think of it as the power, force, personality which is back of everything, and of all our personalities. Scientists speak of this reality as "law" or "evolution."

The modern science of physics has made a purely materialistic conception of the universe impossible. Eddington, Jeans, Stromberg, and a host of other scientists and philosophers, believe that the universe is a creation resulting from the thought of some great

Universal Mind, and that individual minds are related to this Universal Mind in a way similar to the relation of light rays to the sun.

Regardless of the term we use to express this conception, God is the supreme fact of life. It is still true as the German seer Eckhardt once said, "God is at the centre of man."

* * *

Since life is infinite in extent and duration (beyond time and space), there is nothing other than itself upon which it can act. Thus Life acts within itself upon itself.

Personality, likewise, grows and develops by power within itself. Therefore, every individual personality has within itself potential power and capacity for infinite, limitless growth and expansion.

In the light of these considerations, how can that which is inherent and potential in each individual find expression, attainment, achievement? In short, how can this power be used by the individual to get what he needs and wants, to secure favorable conditions of health, employment, happiness, personal security? Can it actually be used by a person, consciously and continuously, to improve his lot in life?

The first consideration to be advanced in reply to these and similar questions has already been stated. Life grows and expands because of power from within. But a test or application of these principles must be made because there is something within the individual which calls for proof. The verification must be sought from within. It cannot be given or received from without. This is the crux of the matter. We must test the reality for ourselves—no one else can do it for us.

Mere logic or reason is not sufficient. What is true for another individual may not be true in our life. Each of us is unique. No single snowflake is ever duplicated, much less a human being. Life is infinite and limitless in its variety. You and I are laws unto ourselves. Of course we do not create the law. Law is fixed and immutable. But we must and do daily determine our *response* to the law—our obedience, our understanding, our use, our application.

As a matter of fact, each of us is testing the law every day. Life in any form is an expression of the principles under discussion. Consider our present condition: Is it one of happiness, prosperity and satisfaction? Or are we frustrated, unhappy, far less successful than we could wish?

In short, are we getting from life what we want?

Whether the answer is Yes or No, we should think of our condition in the light of the conscious control and direction we have achieved to date over our mental and emotional processes or habits.

A little realistic self-analysis will tell us much. As thoughtful persons we must conclude that we have actually built the house in which we live. Is it satisfactory? Will it weather the passing years?

Perhaps we would like to rebuild our house, make it one that will embody elements of durability and security not found in our present house?

Whatever our inclination or decision, the law operates. It is embodied in the make-up of our being. To those who apply it consciously, constructively and intelligently, it is the law of abundant living, of security, poise and satisfaction. To those who do not, life is disappointing. It gives back whatever is put into it.

As already discussed, the foundation stone of any achievement is desire, that which is wanted intensely by the individual. This is the starting point. It is the infinite urge of life—any life—for expression and expansion. Yet surprisingly enough few individuals know what they want. Few ever define, in a concrete, meaningful way, exactly what they ask of life. That most people drift through life rather aimlessly on a day-to-day basis is obvious to us as we witness the failure and frustration in the lives of untold millions of people.

To desire deeply is to be *one-minded*—to team up the surface conscious functioning of our mind with the submerged subconscious. Our success in using the creative power of our mind to get what we want will depend to no small extent on our fitting into the Scheme of Things, of having our mind adjusted to the Infinite Mind, which was described earlier as "the power, force, personality which is back of everything and of all our personalities."

Ralph Waldo Trine summed it up well in a single sentence in a book[1] which made a profound impression on thoughtful people:

"The great central fact in human life, in your life and in mine, is the coming into a conscious, vital realization of our oneness with this Infinite Life, and the opening of ourselves fully to this divine inflow."

[1] From *In Tune with the Infinite,* by Ralph Waldo Trine, copyright 1897, 1933, 1942 and 1947. Used by special permission of the publishers, The Bobbs-Merrill Company, Inc.

None of us can hope to buck the tide of laws and evolutionary processes and make great personal headway. We are dependent not only on our conscious mind but also on the greater submerged subconscious area of our personality; and if we are to realize the fullest, richest life possible, both areas of mind must be tuned to the great universal subconsciousness—The Infinite.

It is when we contemplate this aspect of personal success and achievement that we enter the realm of honor and honesty of purpose, and come face to face with the reality of our social responsibility. To desire for ourselves alone, selfishly and without relation to the rights of others or the welfare of the world we live in, is to fight a tough battle, and perhaps a losing one. Under such circumstances we may be sure the price of getting our way will be exceedingly high.

The final step in the process of personal growth through the creative power of the mind is, therefore, to develop bold, constructive, sustained desire—adjusted to the realities of human welfare and progress, and merged as best we know how into the Scheme of Things.

When we approach life with this attitude, not only

will our subconscious mind become a willing and completely dependable servant, but because we are striving to keep ourselves "in tune with the infinite," we will realize to the fullest possible extent upon our potentialities.

To do this is to live a useful, purposeful and rewarding life.